THE POCKET SCAVENGER

KERI SMITH

PENGUIN BOOKS

Create a funny character.

PENGUIN BOOKS

Published by the Penguin Group
Penguin Books Ltd, 80 Strand, London WC2R 0RL, England
Penguin Group (USA) Inc., 375 Hudson Street, New York, New York 10014, USA
Penguin Group (Canada), 90 Eglinton Avenue East, Suite 700, Toronto, Ontario, Canada M4P 2Y3
(a division of Pearson Penguin Canada Inc.)
Penguin Ireland, 25 St Stephen's Green, Dublin 2, Ireland (a division of Penguin Books Ltd)
Penguin Group (Australia), 707 Collins Street, Melbourne, Victoria 3008, Australia
(a division of Pearson Australia Group Pty Ltd)
Penguin Books India Pvt Ltd, 11 Community Centre, Panchsheel Park, New Delhi – 110 017, India
Penguin Group (NZ), 67 Apollo Drive, Rosedale, Auckland 0632, New Zealand
(a division of Pearson New Zealand Ltd)
Penguin Books (South Africa) (Pty) Ltd, Block D, Rosebank Office Park,
181 Jan Smuts Avenue, Parktown North, Gauteng 2193, South Africa

Penguin Books Ltd, Registered Offices: 80 Strand, London WC2R 0RL, England

www.penguin.com

First published by Perigee Books, part of the Penguin Group (USA) Inc. 2013
First published in Great Britain by Penguin Books 2013
006

Copyright © Keri Smith, 2013

Art and design by Keri Smith

Printed and bound by CPI Group (UK) Ltd, Croydon, CR0 4YY

ISBN: 978-1-846-14709-8

Mixed Sources
Product group from well-managed
forests and recycled wood or fiber
www.fsc.org Cert no. TT-COC-002231
© 1996 Forest Stewardship Council
FSC

Make into a building (house).

THIS BOOK BELONGS TO:

- -

WHO IS AN OFFICIAL SCAVENGER AND
WORLD EXPLORER.

IF FOUND, PLEASE RETURN TO:

- -

(ADDRESS, EMAIL OR PHONE #)

SCAVENGING LOCATIONS:

- - - - - - - - - - - - - - - - - - -

CODENAME: _ _ _ _ _ _ _ _ _ _ _ _ _ _

THIS BOOK IS DEDICATED TO ALL THE
WORLD'S GREAT TEACHERS. IT ONLY
TAKES ONE TO ALTER THE PATH OF A LIFE!

Combine with something from nature.

CONTENTS

INTRODUCTION

COLLECT & ALTER

Turn into a disguise.

Make into a location on a map.

Conceal it.

SOME EXTRA THINGS

Add polka dots.

A SINGLE INANIMATE OBJECT, USELESS IN ITSELF, CAN BE THE FOCUS OF A WORLD.

-YI-FU TUAN

DEFINITION OF A SCAVENGER

Scavengers...

- go on mini adventures no matter where they are, especially in the most mundane of circumstances

- notice the ground beneath their feet, prowl the world looking for treasures

- see beauty in simple items, when sometimes others do not

- know that all objects can be imbued with special powers

- are interested in transforming simple objects into works of art

- often have collections of items in the bottom of their bag, scattered about their home, or hidden in a yard somewhere

- are always prepared to collect and will go to great lengths to do so, even occasionally putting themselves in precarious situations

COULD THIS BE YOU?

If so, proceed to the next section.

Add stripes.

INTRODUCTION

You are invited to go on an adventure—right now, wherever you are.

In the following pages, I'm going to ask you to search for a bunch of items. At first glance, these may seem like simple, mundane, inconsequential things, but don't be fooled—they are of utmost importance!

Every minute of the day there are hundreds (or thousands) of things around us that we don't notice. Our eyes tune them out because they don't seem important for our current needs. But what if we look at every "thing" as if we have never seen it before? As if we do not know its function? In that way, we learn to see it with new eyes.

These things can become very useful if we choose to think of them as raw materials. They are sacred objects just waiting to be collected by a modern-day explorer and used in a variety of artistic experiments.

That is your challenge: to infuse your daily excursions with a quest to see these things with new eyes.

THE
SCAVENGE

The first stage in becoming a natural navigator is to master observation, and the first lesson in this area is that observation is not all about the eyes. And even when it is about the eyes, there is more to it than meets our eyes.
—Tristan Gooley, The Natural Navigator

Most of us have participated in scavenger hunts at some point in our lives: running around a location frantically looking for a set of items typed on a list of some kind, locating the objects before someone else does, finding everything as fast possible.

With the scavenges in this book, we are going to take the act of scavenging into a slightly different realm by first collecting objects and then altering them.

For the first mission, you are going to collect a number of items. They can be found in your immediate environment, on your way to work or school, while you are waiting for the bus, at your local park, while on a hike, while on vacation, and so on. Use the checklist at the back of this book for a quick reference of what to scavenge. For the purposes of this book, you can choose the speed at which you perform the scavenge. You may choose to do it alone. Or you can enlist friends and make it a race.

Fold, cut into pieces, and rearrange.

THE ALTERATION

Once you have an item and are ready for the next step, you will turn the book upside down, flip randomly to a page, read the instruction at the top, and alter the item as instructed. (This is referred to as using "chance" because you do not actively get to choose what alteration you are using. The process of flipping causes you to choose without looking at the alteration first.)

These alterations will allow you to create something entirely new. Think of them as a selection of possibilities for outcomes different than what you would have done if you were given a choice. The alterations are where your genius will come in. Each alteration will be interpreted differently by each person. There is no right or wrong or good or bad in terms of how the alteration is performed. You might love the results; you might find them uninteresting. That is part of the fun—not knowing what will occur.

Turn into an article of clothing.

CHANCE:

1. the occurrence and development of events in the absence of any obvious design : he met his brother by chance | what a lucky chance that you are here 2. the unplanned and unpredictable course of events regarded as a power : chance was offering me success.

A BRIEF HISTORY OF CHANCE

The use of chance in art began in the 1950s with the artists Ellsworth Kelly, François Morellet, and John Cage. These artists used a variety of methods and techniques including the I Ching, grid systems (assigning random colors to the squares), dot systems, random sampling on a computer, dice, using gravity (falling, dropping, dripping), chance meetings, etc.

Trace it and use the shape as basis for a new drawing.

So often when we are creating something—a piece of art, a piece of writing, a musical composition—we do what has worked for us in the past, what we are the best at, what is current, what is reliable, what is obvious, what we think is good. But this method tends to make our work repetitive and stale. Creativity arises from our ability to see things from many different angles. New connections (things that have not been connected before) create new ideas.

Incorporating chance into the exercise allows us to make connections and try things that we might not have done on our own. We are forced out of our habitual ways of thinking or acting.

Chance is beloved of Art, and Art of Chance.

–Agathon, fragments (c. 415 B.C.), quoted by Aristotle

THE BENEFITS AND JOYS OF BEING A SCAVENGER

I devote a day to creating a kind of "story." Walking down, say, Sixth Avenue, I'll suddenly see something that intrigues me—a plastic bag, a green umbrella, an airplane tracing a line in the sky. That's how I get started.
—Gabriel Orozco (on recent films, 1998)

1. The process of collecting tunes us into our environment and makes use of our increasingly underused senses. You may begin to see that everything is interesting.

2. In our current culture of immediacy, we have lost the experience of "the quest," the search for that elusive item and the stories we create in our attempt to find it. These stories, the process (vs. the object itself), are often what make life interesting.

3. Scavenging is fun and addictive (and much better for us than watching screens all day), especially when done with others and when you share your unique results.

4. Living in a consumerist society, it is easy to get caught up in a lifestyle that is just about shopping or is connected to a corporate entity. This leaves us feeling empty and causes a discon-

Combine with page 14.

nect with the natural world. It is important for us to participate in activities that open us up to exploring the world around us on a regular basis without a focus on money/commerce. Tuning into our immediate environment also serves to make us feel more connected to the natural world.

5. You will never be at a loss for materials for artistic endeavors.

What if we begin to see the world as alive and animate? What if every item told a story?

With The Pocket Scavenger, what emerges will be entirely different for every person who works with the book. Each version will be based on a variety of factors, our life experiences, our location, our culture, chance, and how we interpret the ideas. Working with items in this way will help train our brains to look at things without preconceived ideas. Over time we will naturally make new connections and formulate new patterns of thinking. We will develop a habit of "trying something new" or different.

AN IMPORTANT NOTE:

SOMETIMES THE RESULT WILL BE INTERESTING AND SOMETIMES IT WON'T. THAT IS THE NATURE OF AN EXPERIMENT.

Clean it up.

SCAVENGER TOOLS

YOU WILL NEED:

ERASER CHALK SCISSOR

PAINT

A VARIETY OF WRITING AND DRAWING UTENSILS

A SELECTION OF ART MATERIALS

COFFEE TEA

SAND PAPER

NEWSPAPER MUD

SOME NON-ART MATERIALS*

* SEE LIST OF ALTERATION MATERIALS ON THE NEXT PAGE.

VARIOUS WAYS TO STORE THINGS UNTIL YOU CAN AFFIX THEM INTO THE BOOK. ATTACH AN ENVELOPE TO THE INSIDE OF THE BACK COVER TO STORE THINGS TEMPORARILY WHEN YOU ARE OUT ON SCAVENGES.

Add a mess.

A "SCAVENGING UNIFORM" OF SOME KIND, SOMETHING THAT HELPS GET YOU INTO THE MIND-SET.

SCAVENGING HAT

OLD SWEATER WITH POCKETS

BAG

FAVORITE WALKING BOOTS

CAMERA (OPTIONAL)

UMBRELLA (OPTIONAL)

Turn it upside down. What does it look like now?

ATTACHMENT METHODS:

GLUE

PAPER CLIP

SEWING

STAPLER

TAPE

WHEAT PASTE
(MADE OUT OF
FLOUR & WATER)

PINS

STICKERS

NOTE: SOME ITEMS MAY SEEM A LITTLE BULKY FOR THE BOOK. THIS IS TO BE EXPECTED. YOU MAY HAVE TO PUT A LARGE ELASTIC BAND AROUND IT TO KEEP IT CONTAINED.

ALTERATION MATERIALS YOU MAY LIKE TO USE...

HAMMER
SCISSORS
PAINT BRUSH
PEN
PENCIL
PIN
INK
WATER BASED PAINT
WATER
CHARCOAL

STICKS
WHITE GLUE
TAPE
CRAYONS
PAPER
FOUND PHOTO
COFFEE/TEA
PAPER BAG

FOOD
SANDPAPER
STONES
CHALK
STRAW
MAGAZINE OR NEWSPAPER
PUSH PINS
ELASTIC BAND
MARKERS

LEAVES
PLASTIC BAGS
DIRT
CARDBOARD
CEREAL
FABRIC
STRING
ERASER
ASH
*ANYTHING ELSE YOU CAN THINK OF.
COIN

SCAVENGING TIPS

- Get in the habit of looking around while wandering in your neighborhood. Scan the ground for finds. Some things you will find quickly, or know exactly where to look. Others will take some time and require ingenuity and serendipity. Occasionally you will come upon something when you least expect it (e.g., while walking to work, you spot a piece of red string on the sidewalk); these are the most interesting finds and make the best stories. Write about it on the object's page.

- Recruit your friends and family to help you (if you choose).

- Enjoy the process. Scavenging works best when you are fully immersed in the moment.

- Memorize (or familiarize) yourself with the list of items to scavenge, so you will be working on it as you go about your day.

- Try navigating your environment in a non-linear fashion, or take different routes than you normally do. You may discover new things this way.

  IMPORTANT NOTE: You will want to avoid any items that are sharp, dangerous-looking, or toxic. (Avoid standing water or unknown substances.) If you are unsure if an item is okay, it is best to leave it behind.

Add some kind of explosion.

ALTERATION TIPS

- Be willing to try something just to see what happens—even if you don't think you will like it. You may come up with the most interesting stuff this way! Get into the habit of experimenting.

- If you come upon a wild card you may pick an alteration of your choosing, or you can just flip again.

- Try working with as many different materials as you can. So for example, if the alteration says "add dots" you could use paint, coffee, gum, collage, or anything else you can think of!

- If you are prone to cheating, dare yourself to do as instructed.

- If you really dislike what you created, you have permission to repeat the whole process or transform it into something else entirely.

Bonus tip: You may like to use the alterations in this book for other projects you are working on.

Add warmth.

INSTRUCTIONS

1. Take this book with you everywhere you go.

2. Find/collect the things on each page. Affix them some-how to the left-hand side of the page.* Fill in the notes about where you found the item. Under "story" you can describe the circumstances surrounding the scavenge.** You may also choose to write an imaginary story about the item.

3. For each collected item, turn the book upside down and randomly flip to a page. Alter it as directed. How you inter-pret each alteration is up to you.

4. Share your alterations with others using your preferred method (social network, art show, trade book with friends, etc.).

*You may also choose to take photos of the items, but you must find a way to print them so you can alter them later.

**Remember that these items may not seem that important on their own, but in your collecting of them, they will be-come valuable treasures. You will become the envy of all your friends!

Group several items together.

SCAVENGER MAP

Draw a detailed map of your neighborhood. Document on the map all of the locations at which you found your scavenged items. Create your own legend.

Destroy it.

LEGEND

It's a hat.

POSTAGE STAMPS

CALL ME TRIMTAB

LOCATION FOUND: _____

TIME: _____ DATE: _____

STORY: _____

_____

_____

_____

_____

_____

_____

_____

_____

_____

_____

_____

_____

Flip three pages ahead—follow those directions.

② THE NUMBER FIVE

5

LOCATION FOUND: _____

TIME: _____ DATE: _____

STORY: _____

_____

_____

_____

_____

_____

_____

_____

_____

_____

_____

_____

_____

_____

_____

Alter the edges.

Make item the background for something else.

3
PAPER CLIP

LOCATION FOUND:_____

TIME:_____ DATE:_____

STORY:_____

_____

_____

_____

_____

_____

_____

_____

_____

_____

_____

Wild card. Choose an alteration yourself.

Add some texture.

4

A FEATHER

LOCATION FOUND: _____

TIME: _____ DATE: _____

STORY: _____

_____

_____

_____

_____

_____

_____

_____

_____

_____

_____

_____

Make holes.

Ask a friend what you should do.

5
A USED
ENVELOPE

LOCATION FOUND:_____

TIME:_____ DATE:_____

STORY:_____

_____

_____

_____

_____

_____

_____

_____

_____

_____

_____

_____

_____

_____

Add legs.

6

A TICKET

INSTRUCTIONS

CLAIM # 978-1-59017-313-

LOCATION FOUND:_____

TIME:_____ DATE:_____

STORY:_____

_____

_____

_____

_____

_____

_____

_____

_____

_____

_____

Combine with a photo.

Add ten colors.

7
NINE CIRCLES

LOCATION FOUND:_____

TIME:_____ DATE:_____

STORY:_____

_____

_____

_____

_____

_____

_____

_____

_____

_____

_____

_____

Invent an animal.

Make a self-portrait.

8

A FORM OF CURRENCY

LOCATION FOUND: _____

TIME: _____ DATE: _____

STORY: _____

_____

_____

_____

_____

_____

_____

_____

_____

_____

_____

_____

_____

_____

_____

Alter the space around the item (not the item itself).

Add a series of diverging lines.

SOMETHING YOU
CAN SEE THROUGH

LOCATION FOUND:_____

TIME:_____ DATE:_____

STORY:_____

_____

_____

_____

_____

_____

_____

_____

_____

_____

_____

Add a color you dislike.

Fill the entire space.

10
THREE DIFFERENT TEXTURES

LOCATION FOUND:_____

TIME:_____ DATE:_____

STORY:_____

_____

_____

_____

_____

_____

_____

_____

_____

_____

_____

_____

Add transparent/translucent layers.

12

A POST-IT NOTE

The magician's underwear has just been found in a cardboard suitcase floating in a stagnant pond on the outskirts of

LOCATION FOUND:_____

TIME:_____ DATE:_____

STORY:_____

_____

_____

_____

_____

_____

_____

_____

_____

_____

_____

_____

Smudge something over it with your fingers.

Crumple it.

II

SOMETHING
WITH TEXT
ON IT

READ
THIS.

LOCATION FOUND:_____

TIME:_____ DATE:_____

STORY:_____

_____

_____

_____

_____

_____

_____

_____

_____

_____

_____

_____

_____

Delete the middle.

Do something your hero would do.

14
SOME WIRE

LOCATION FOUND:_____
TIME:_____ DATE:_____
STORY:_____
_____
_____
_____
_____
_____
_____
_____
_____
_____
_____

Add a series of triangles.

Turn into a landscape.

13

A PIECE OF MOSS

LOCATION FOUND:_____

TIME:_____ DATE:_____

STORY:_____

_____

_____

_____

_____

_____

_____

_____

_____

_____

_____

Soak with water.

Add scratches.

16

SOMETHING YOU CAN ONLY FIND IN YOUR LOCAL ENVIRONMENT

LOCATION FOUND:_____

TIME:_____ DATE:_____

STORY:_____

_____

_____

_____

_____

_____

_____

_____

_____

_____

_____

Lose the item.

Drip coffee or tea on it.

15

A PART OF SOMETHING YOU ATE

LOCATION FOUND:_____

TIME:_____ DATE:_____

STORY:_____

_____

_____

_____

_____

_____

_____

_____

_____

_____

_____

Draw a box.

Place in a location where it will get dirty.

18

A USED TEA BAG

RECEIPT
0-679-
42299-9

LOCATION FOUND:_____
TIME:_____ DATE:_____
STORY:_____

_____

_____

_____

_____

_____

_____

_____

_____

_____

_____

Chop it up.

17

SOMETHING ON YOUR BODY

LOCATION FOUND:_____

TIME:_____ DATE:_____

STORY:_____

_____

_____

_____

_____

_____

_____

_____

_____

_____

Drip paint on it.

19

A NAPKIN

LOCATION FOUND:_____

TIME:_____ DATE:_____

STORY:_____

_____

_____

_____

_____

_____

_____

_____

_____

_____

_____

_____

Make it political.

Make it obscured.

20

HELLO
MY NAME IS:

SOMETHING STICKY

LOCATION FOUND:_____

TIME:_____ DATE:_____

STORY:_____

_____

_____

_____

_____

_____

_____

_____

_____

_____

_____

_____

Add string.

Turn it into something else.

21

SIX BLUE THINGS

LOCATION FOUND:_____

TIME:_____ DATE:_____

STORY:_____

_____

_____

_____

_____

_____

_____

_____

_____

_____

_____

_____

_____

Change the perspective.

22
A PIECE OF
A PUZZLE

LOCATION FOUND:_____

TIME:_____ DATE:_____

STORY:_____

_____

_____

_____

_____

_____

_____

_____

_____

_____

_____

Drag it along a rough surface.

Smear something onto it.

23

AN ELASTIC BAND

LOCATION FOUND:_____
TIME:_____ DATE:_____
STORY:_____
_____
_____
_____
_____
_____
_____
_____
_____
_____
_____
_____

Cut out some bits of paper. Glue them on.

Add some thumbprints.

24

AN IMAGE OF A CHARACTER

LOCATION FOUND:_____

TIME:_____   DATE:_____

STORY:_____

_____

_____

_____

_____

_____

_____

_____

_____

_____

_____

Add circles.

Draw the opposite.

25

SEVERAL KINDS OF LEAVES

LOCATION FOUND:_____

TIME:_____ DATE:_____

STORY:_____

_____

_____

_____

_____

_____

_____

_____

_____

_____

_____

_____

_____

26
A PIECE OF
RED STRING

LOCATION FOUND:_____

TIME:_____ DATE:_____

STORY:_____

_____

_____

_____

_____

_____

_____

_____

_____

_____

_____

What sound would it make?

27

A WRAPPER

LOCATION FOUND:_____

TIME:_____ DATE:_____

STORY:_____

_____

_____

_____

_____

_____

_____

_____

_____

_____

Age it.

28

A PHOTO OF YOURSELF

LOCATION FOUND:_____

TIME:_____ DATE:_____

STORY:_____

_____

_____

_____

_____

_____

_____

_____

_____

_____

_____

Wild card. Choose an alteration yourself.

Add eyes.

29

A POSTCARD

LOCATION FOUND:_____

TIME:_____ DATE:_____

STORY:_____

_____

_____

_____

_____

_____

_____

_____

_____

_____

_____

_____

Add tape.

Color outside the lines.

30

FOUR SQUARES

LOCATION FOUND:_____

TIME:_____ DATE:_____

STORY:_____

_____

_____

_____

_____

_____

_____

_____

_____

_____

_____

_____

Make it REALLY funny.

31

FIVE BUTTONS

LOCATION FOUND:_____

TIME:_____ DATE:_____

STORY:_____

_____

_____

_____

_____

_____

_____

_____

_____

_____

_____

Turn it into a math equation.

Turn it into a pattern (repeat it).

32
AN IMAGE OF AN ELEPHANT

LOCATION FOUND: _____

TIME: _____ DATE: _____

STORY: _____

_____

_____

_____

_____

_____

_____

_____

_____

_____

_____

Add a newspaper clipping.

33

ROCK TRACINGS

LOCATION FOUND:_____

TIME:_____ DATE:_____

STORY:_____

_____

_____

_____

_____

_____

_____

_____

_____

_____

_____

_____

_____

_____

_____

_____

_____

_____

_____

Stencil something over top (a word or a shape).

34
SOMETHING ORANGE

LOCATION FOUND:_____

TIME:_____ DATE:_____

STORY:_____

_____

_____

_____

_____

_____

_____

_____

_____

_____

Add fog.

Add exactly six lines/marks.

35

SOMETHING FROM THE YEAR YOU WERE BORN

LOCATION FOUND:_____

TIME:_____ DATE:_____

STORY:_____

_____

_____

_____

_____

_____

_____

_____

_____

_____

Add a grid.

Cover with chalk. Remove some.

36

A HANDWRITTEN QUOTE

LOCATION FOUND:_____

TIME:_____ DATE:_____

STORY:_____

_____

_____

_____

_____

_____

_____

_____

_____

Play.

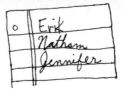

SAMPLES OF HANDWRITING FROM FIVE DIFFERENT PEOPLE

LOCATION FOUND:_____

TIME:_____ DATE:_____

STORY:_____

_____

_____

_____

_____

_____

_____

_____

_____

_____

_____

_____

_____

_____

_____

Add one never-ending line.

38

A PENCIL RUBBING OF A GRAVESTONE

LOCATION FOUND:_____

TIME:_____ DATE:_____

STORY:_____

_____

_____

_____

_____

_____

_____

_____

_____

_____

_____

_____

_____

_____

_____

_____

_____

_____

What memory does it spark? Write about it.

75

Turn into an adventure.

39

A HAIR SAMPLE

LOCATION FOUND:_____

TIME:_____ DATE:_____

STORY:_____

_____

_____

_____

_____

_____

_____

_____

_____

_____

_____

Add a shadow.

Write five questions about the item.

40

YOU WILL SOON MAKE A FRIEND.

A FORTUNE FROM A FORTUNE COOKIE

LOCATION FOUND:_____

TIME:_____ DATE:_____

STORY:_____

_____

_____

_____

_____

_____

_____

_____

_____

_____

_____

_____

_____

Add some very tiny, almost imperceptible decoration.

Turn into a badge.

41

A COUPON

COUPON
#0-14-130115-5
GREETINGS TO YOU, THE
LUCKY FINDER OF THIS COUPON.

LOCATION FOUND:_____

TIME:_____ DATE:_____

STORY:_____

_____

_____

_____

_____

_____

_____

_____

_____

_____

_____

_____

_____

Turn into a magical object.

Wild card. Choose an alteration yourself.

42

SOMETHING THAT IS BROKEN OR DAMAGED

LOCATION FOUND:_____

TIME:_____ DATE:_____

STORY:_____

_____

_____

_____

_____

_____

_____

_____

_____

Invent a story.

dd a color based on a memory association with the item.

43

SOMETHING THAT WAS DISCARDED

CITY LIGHTS BOOKS

OPEN EVERYDAY 10AM TO
A LITERARY MEETINGPLACE MIDNIGHT
SINCE 1953.

DHARMA BUMS - 6.95
THE REAL WORK 8.95

SUBTOTAL   15.90
TAX   1.35
TOTAL   17.25

EXCHANGE ONLY W/
RECEIPT W/IN 7 DAYS

LOCATION FOUND:_____

TIME:_____ DATE:_____

STORY:_____

_____

_____

_____

_____

_____

_____

_____

_____

_____

_____

Write an ode to this item.

44

A STAIN MADE BY A LIQUID

LOCATION FOUND:_____

TIME:_____ DATE:_____

STORY:_____

_____

_____

_____

_____

_____

_____

_____

_____

_____

Add your favorite color in abundance.

45

A STAIN THAT IS GREEN

LOCATION FOUND:_____

TIME:_____ DATE:_____

STORY:_____

_____

_____

_____

_____

_____

_____

_____

_____

_____

_____

Alter item in a way that makes you happy.

Add a pattern.

46

SOMETHING THAT CAN BE CRUMBLED

LOCATION FOUND:_____

TIME:_____ DATE:_____

STORY:_____

_____

_____

_____

_____

_____

_____

_____

_____

Turn into a floorplan.

Combine with a leaf.

47
SOMETHING THAT CAN BE DRAGGED AND LEAVES A MARK

LOCATION FOUND:_____

TIME:_____ DATE:_____

STORY:_____

_____

_____

_____

_____

_____

_____

_____

_____

_____

Add some cracks.

Add stitches.

48

SOMETHING THAT WAS PART OF A TREE

LOCATION FOUND:_____

TIME:_____ DATE:_____

STORY:_____

_____

_____

_____

_____

_____

_____

_____

_____

_____

_____

Add some triangles.

Make it inviting.

49

SOMETHING THAT WAS PLANTED

LOCATION FOUND:_____

TIME:_____ DATE:_____

STORY:_____

_____

_____

_____

_____

_____

_____

_____

_____

_____

Connect this item to an item you love.

50

A FOUND NOTE

LOCATION FOUND:_____

TIME:_____ DATE:_____

STORY:_____

_____

_____

_____

_____

_____

_____

_____

_____

_____

Dream up a scenario.

Take in a different direction.

51

A PIECE OF FLAT CANDY

LOCATION FOUND:_____

TIME:_____ DATE:_____

STORY:_____

_____

_____

_____

_____

_____

_____

_____

_____

_____

_____

_____

What would you have done at age five?

Add another dimension.

52

A FEW SEED PODS

LOCATION FOUND: _____

TIME: _____ DATE: _____

STORY: _____

_____

_____

_____

_____

_____

_____

_____

_____

_____

Rearrange.

Drip and blow ink.

53

SOMETHING LEFT BY AN ANIMAL

LOCATION FOUND:_____

TIME:_____ DATE:_____

STORY:_____

_____

_____

_____

_____

_____

_____

_____

_____

_____

_____

Cut in half.

54

Drink Me!

SOMETHING THAT WAS CREATED USING A MACHINE

LOCATION FOUND:_____

TIME:_____ DATE:_____

STORY:_____

_____

_____

_____

_____

_____

_____

_____

_____

_____

_____

_____

Paint with your finger.

Drop string that has ink on it (make a print).

55

SOMETHING THAT WAS MADE BY HAND

LOCATION FOUND: _____

TIME: _____ DATE: _____

STORY: _____

_____

_____

_____

_____

_____

_____

_____

_____

_____

_____

_____

Rub surface with dirt.

Squirt ink (or another colored liquid).

56

SOMETHING THAT IS MINIATURE

LOCATION FOUND:_____

TIME:_____ DATE:_____

STORY:_____

_____

_____

_____

_____

_____

_____

_____

_____

_____

_____

Add several blobs of glue.

57

A PIECE OF ORIGAMI

LOCATION FOUND:_____

TIME:_____ DATE:_____

STORY:_____

_____

_____

_____

_____

_____

_____

_____

_____

_____

_____

_____

_____

_____

_____

Wild card. Choose an alteration yourself.

Turn into a monster.

58

SOMETHING THAT WAS GIVEN TO YOU

LOCATION FOUND:_____

TIME:_____ DATE:_____

STORY:_____

_____

_____

_____

_____

_____

_____

_____

_____

_____

_____

Add a pencil rubbing texture.

60

SEVERAL DIFFERENT KINDS OF GRASS

LOCATION FOUND:_____

TIME:_____ DATE:_____

STORY:_____

_____

_____

_____

_____

_____

_____

_____

_____

_____

Alter the shape.

Print something onto it.

59

A DRAWING (NOT DONE BY YOU)

LOCATION FOUND:_____

TIME:_____ DATE:_____

STORY:_____

_____

_____

_____

_____

_____

_____

_____

_____

_____

_____

_____

Add something that is blown across the surface.

120

62

A PIECE OF STYROFOAM

LOCATION FOUND:_____

TIME:_____ DATE:_____

STORY:_____

_____

_____

_____

_____

_____

_____

_____

_____

_____

_____

_____

_____

Turn it into a machine/device.

61
SOMETHING THAT IS IMAGINARY

LOCATION FOUND:_____

TIME:_____ DATE:_____

STORY:_____

_____

_____

_____

_____

_____

_____

_____

_____

_____

_____

_____

Make it into a boat.

Combine several alterations of your choosing.

64

SOMETHING WITH SPOTS

LOCATION FOUND:_____

TIME:_____ DATE:_____

STORY:_____

_____

_____

_____

_____

_____

_____

_____

_____

_____

Draw in the same direction as the wind.

63

SEVERAL PLASTIC ITEMS OF DIFFERENT COLORS

LOCATION FOUND:_____

TIME:_____ DATE:_____

STORY:_____

_____

_____

_____

_____

_____

_____

_____

_____

_____

_____

Add a grid.

SIX TRIANGLES

LOCATION FOUND:_____

TIME:_____ DATE:_____

STORY:_____

_____

_____

_____

_____

_____

_____

_____

_____

_____

_____

_____

_____

65

SOMETHING CURVED

LOCATION FOUND:_____

TIME:_____ DATE:_____

STORY:_____

_____

_____

_____

_____

_____

_____

_____

_____

_____

Add colored paper.

Do some crosshatching.

SOMETHING WITH A HOLE IN IT

LOCATION FOUND:_____

TIME:_____ DATE:_____

STORY:_____

_____

_____

_____

_____

_____

_____

_____

_____

_____

Add your favorite shape.

68

A PART OF A BOOK

LOCATION FOUND:_____

TIME:_____ DATE:_____

STORY:_____

_____

_____

_____

_____

_____

_____

_____

_____

_____

Add something orange.

Combine with an everyday object.

69

A PENCIL RUBBING OF THE BOTTOM OF A SHOE

LOCATION FOUND:_____

TIME:_____ DATE:_____

STORY:_____

_____

_____

_____

_____

_____

_____

_____

_____

_____

_____

_____

Do something you never do.

70

SOMETHING FROM A CONSTRUCTION SITE

LOCATION FOUND:_____

TIME:_____ DATE:_____

STORY:_____

_____

_____

_____

_____

_____

_____

_____

_____

_____

Turn it into something else.

Re-create it in another material.

9 780671 696588 0

0-671-69588-6

A UPC SYMBOL

LOCATION FOUND:_____

TIME:_____   DATE:_____

STORY:_____

_____

_____

_____

_____

_____

_____

_____

_____

_____

_____

_____

Place it into a new environment.

72
A PIECE OF GREEN FABRIC

LOCATION FOUND: _____

TIME: _____ DATE: _____

STORY: _____

_____

_____

_____

_____

_____

_____

_____

_____

_____

_____

_____

_____

_____

Add clouds.

Smudge pencil lines with your finger.

144

SOME EXTRA THINGS

(FURTHER SCAVENGING)

FUN THINGS TO DO

•Play a game with two or more people. Assign an item for every-one to collect. Then have everyone use the same alteration. Impose a time limit for the alteration. Compare results.

•Try doing several alterations to each item. You may wish to roll a die to tell you how many alterations to employ.

•Try completing all of the collecting at once, and then begin the alterations.

•Try collecting multiples of one of the items and experimenting with many different alterations (or combinations of alterations).

•Make an exhibit with your items. Create a mini museum in a public forum.

•Start a scavenger flash mob. Invite people to do a public scaven-ger hunt on a social network.

•Create your own scavenges. Hide things for a friend to find on their way to school/work.

•Conduct a scavenging workshop, or create a club. Pick a new item to find every week.

•Take the things you have collected and explore them further. Conduct research. Trace the origins. Look at them from many different perspectives, shape, color, texture, history, etc. Pretend you are new to the planet. What do these items tell you about the inhabitants of earth?

•Take your altered items and create some kind of narrative based on them.

•Experiment with the scavenges on the following pages.

Give it an interesting title or caption.

Turn it into a mask.

RANDOM

SCAVENGE

1. Take a walk in your neighborhood.

2. Collect twenty things you find on your walk.

3. Document them on a map. Write a story about each item.

CARDBOARD

KEY RING

TAG

STONE WITH LINE ON IT

BLUE RIBBON

UPC CODE

GRASS

ACORN CAP

BUTTON

GREEN LEAF

Combine with another object.

QUICK SCAVENGE

Collect ten things in ten minutes.

SOUND
SCAVENGE

Using some kind of sound recorder, record ten different sounds you hear in your environment.

If you do not have a sound recorder you can make up different symbols for the sounds you hear and mark them on a map or graph.

SKETCH BOOK

10

Add something shiny.

SKETCH SCAVENGE

1. Go for a walk in a predetermined location.

2. Sketch ten items you find.

3. Document the locations on a map.

Add a crooked line.

A b c D E
f G h i j K
L m R N O P
Q R S t U
V W X y Z

Add a blob.

ALPHABET SCAVENGE

You must find and document the whole alphabet while out on a walk. You will need to use a camera for this.

Find and add something with a similar shape.

2. Collect as many different kinds of wild plants as you can. (Make sure to avoid poison oak and stinging nettles!) (Note: If it is a place where the flora and fauna are protected, such as a state park, then document with photos.) It may be helpful to use a plant identification guidebook.

3. Arrange your collection and try to identify the plants using a field guide.

Build it up.

Build it up with layers.

MAP
SCAVENGE

1. Choose a specific location with defined boundaries (park, street block).

2. Go for a walk and choose ten objects/landmarks.

3. Create a set of clues for each thing (for example, next to the red fire hydrant, something that is yellow).

4. Give the clues to a friend and have your friend locate each item.

Wild card. Choose an alteration yourself.

Create your own alteration.

STAINS AND SPILLS

Go out and document as many stains or spills as you can. (You could also include discarded gum or shapes made by water.)

Fill every square inch with something.

ONE THING
SCAVENGE

1. Choose one object to collect or document. (Some ideas: blue things, rubber bands, tickets, stamps, park benches, etc.)

2. Look for the object everywhere you go. Collect or document it in some way.

Go crazy on it.

HANDSPUN WOOL

DRIFTWOOD

COLORED PLASTIC BITS

OLD PAPER

LINEN

LEATHER

ROCKS

ROPE

TEA

PERSONAL SCAVENGE

1. Create a scavenge based on your own personal preferences and tastes (for example, find a wrapper from your favorite candy, find a variety of textures you really enjoy).

2. Give it to a friend to use.

Go away for five minutes. Come back and doodle something

167

Add as many things as you can.

PLASTIC SCAVENGE

1. Collect as many pieces of discarded plastic as you can.

2. Document them separately or as a group.

3. Create some kind of installation with the pieces.

Make part of it pretty and part of it ugly.

MEETING PLACE: THE PARK

SCAVENGE

YOU MUST FIND:

1 CANDY WRAPPER
1 PENNY
4 LEAVES
2 NEWSPAPER CLIPPINGS
1 CRAB APPLE
1 PIECE OF BARK
1 PIECE OF PLASTIC
1 BLADE OF GRASS
1 SAMPLE OF HANDWRITING
2 ACORN HATS

Assemble some art materials. Use them all.

MEETING SCAVENGE

1. Arrange to meet a friend at a specific location.

2. Each person gives a scavenge assignment to the other to collect a predetermined number of objects.

LUCY WAS HERE.

SAM 2001

URBAN
FOSSILS

Go out and document as many urban fossils as you can find. These will be things that have been embedded somehow in concrete sidewalks—footprints (animal and human), leaf prints, patterns, coins, names, etc.

CHECKLIST

QUICK REFERENCE LIST OF ITEMS

- [ ] POSTAGE STAMPS
- [ ] THE NUMBER FIVE
- [ ] A PAPER CLIP
- [ ] A FEATHER
- [ ] A USED ENVELOPE
- [ ] A TICKET
- [ ] NINE CIRCLES
- [ ] CURRENCY
- [ ] SEE THROUGH
- [ ] THREE DIFFERENT TEXTURES
- [ ] TEXT
- [ ] A POST-IT NOTE
- [ ] A PIECE OF MOSS
- [ ] SOME WIRE
- [ ] SOMETHING YOU ATE
- [ ] LOCAL ENVIRONMENT
- [ ] ON YOUR BODY
- [ ] A USED TEA BAG
- [ ] A NAPKIN
- [ ] SOMETHING STICKY
- [ ] SIX BLUE THINGS
- [ ] PUZZLE PIECE
- [ ] AN ELASTIC BAND
- [ ] CHARACTER
- [ ] SEVERAL LEAVES

- [ ] RED STRING
- [ ] A WRAPPER
- [ ] A PHOTO OF YOURSELF
- [ ] A POSTCARD
- [ ] FOUR SQUARES
- [ ] FIVE BUTTONS
- [ ] ELEPHANT
- [ ] ROCK TRACINGS
- [ ] SOMETHING ORANGE
- [ ] YEAR YOU WERE BORN
- [ ] HANDWRITTEN QUOTE
- [ ] FIVE SAMPLES HANDWRITING
- [ ] GRAVESTONE RUBBING
- [ ] A HAIR SAMPLE
- [ ] FORTUNE
- [ ] COUPON
- [ ] SOMETHING BROKEN
- [ ] SOMETHING DISCARDED
- [ ] LIQUID STAIN
- [ ] GREEN STAIN
- [ ] SOMETHING CRUMBLED
- [ ] SOMETHING DRAGGED
- [ ] PART OF A TREE
- [ ] SOMETHING PLANTED

- [ ] A FOUND NOTE
- [ ] FLAT CANDY
- [ ] SEED PODS
- [ ] LEFT BY AN ANIMAL
- [ ] MACHINE MADE
- [ ] HANDMADE
- [ ] MINIATURE
- [ ] ORIGAMI
- [ ] GIVEN TO YOU
- [ ] DRAWING
- [ ] GRASS
- [ ] IMAGINARY
- [ ] STYROFOAM
- [ ] PLASTIC
- [ ] SPOTS
- [ ] SOMETHING CURVED
- [ ] SIX TRIANGLES
- [ ] HOLE IN IT
- [ ] PART OF A BOOK
- [ ] BOTTOM OF SHOE
- [ ] CONSTRUCTION SITE
- [ ] UPC SYMBOL
- [ ] GREEN FABRIC

Turn it into something that flies.

175

What would it say if it could talk?

THIS PAGE IS RESERVED
FOR A MYSTERY OBJECT*

* AN OBJECT YOU FIND WHILE ON A SCAVENGE THAT IS NOT ON THE LIST BUT IS TOO GOOD TO PASS UP.

LOCATION FOUND:_____

TIME:_____   DATE:_____

STORY:_____

_____

_____

_____

_____

_____

_____

_____

_____

Add a paper bag.

BIBLIOGRAPHY

Abram, David. The Spell of the Sensuous. New York: Vintage, 1997.

Bachelard, Gaston. The Poetics of Space. Boston: Beacon Press, 1994.

Buchanan-Smith, Peter. Speck: A Curious Collection of Uncommon Things. New York: Princeton Architectural Press, 2001.

Elpel, Thomas J. Botany in a Day: The Patterns Method of Plant Identification. Pony, Montana: HOPS Press, 2004.

Fletcher, Allan. The Art of Looking Sideways. New York: Phaidon Press, 2001.

Fletcher, Allan. Picturing and Poeting. New York: Phaidon Press, 2006.

Gooley, Tristan. The Natural Navigator. New York: The Experiment, 2010.

Harmon, Katherine. You Are Here: Personal Geographies and Other Maps of the Imagination. New York: Princeton Architectural Press, 2003.

Jernigan, Candy. Evidence: The Art of Candy Jernigan. San Francisco: Chronicle Books, 1999.

Create a collage.

Johnstone, Stephen (editor). <u>The Everyday</u>. Boston: MIT Press, 2008.

Kent, Corita. <u>Learning by Heart</u>. Allworth Press: 2008.

Munari, Bruno. <u>From Afar It Was an Island</u>. Verona, Italy: Corraini, 1971.

Munari, Bruno. <u>The Sea as Craftsman</u>. Mantova Italy, 1995.

Munari, Bruno. <u>The Tactile Workshops</u>. Mantova Italy, 1985.

Perec, Georges. <u>The Species of Spaces and Other Pieces</u>. New York: Penguin, 2008.

Tuan, Yi-Fu. <u>Space and Place: The Perspective of Experience</u>. Boston: Beacon Press, 1994.

Wilde, Ann and Jürgen Wilde (editors). <u>Karl Blossfeldt: Working Collages</u>. Boston: MIT Press, 2001.

Documentary Films

<u>The Gleaners and I</u> by Agnès Varda

<u>Waste Land</u> by Lucy Walker, João Jardim, and Karen Harley

Invite a bunch of friends.

ALSO FROM KERI SMITH

PARTICULAR BOOKS
an imprint of
PENGUIN BOOKS

T258-0213

Add the sun.

180